FAMOUS NORTHERN BATTLES

by
Frank Graham

Front Cover: Battle of Otterburn by Ronald Embleton

ISBN 0 946928 21 5

First published by Frank Graham
Published by Butler Publishing 1988
This reprint 1995

Butler Publishing
Rothbury Northumberland

Printed by Crescent Printing Company
195 Alexandra Road, Ashington, Northumberland NE63 9LA

THE BATTLE OF HEAVENFIELD (635 A.D.)

In the fourth decade of the seventh century the Christian kingdom of Northumbria was engaged in a life and death struggle with the Welsh under their king Cadwallon. The first great battle took place in 633 at Heathfield (Hatfield) near Doncaster which ended in the death of King Edwin and the destruction of his army. A great part of Northumbria was then laid waste and pillaged. The task of saving the kingdom fell upon Oswald, the second son of Ethelfrith, who had been trained by the Celtic monks of Scotland.

Collecting a small army he met the victorious Cadwallon near Hexham. He chose as the site for the battle a plateau, protected to the north and west by rocky banks and to the south by the Roman Wall. Bede – who wrote when the battle was still vividly remembered – tells us that Oswald erected a cross of wood as a standard for his army. Then he led his men in prayer; kneeling at the foot of the cross he said: "Let us all bow the knee, and together pray the Almighty God, living and true, that He will in His mercy save us from the proud and savage enemy, as He knows that we have undertaken a just war for the salvation of our nation." They then awaited the onslaught of the foe. In the bitter conflict the Welsh were utterly routed and their king slain. "Never was day more lamentable for the Britons, or more joyful for the Angles", as the chronicler said.

The Britons fled down Watling Street and it was at the Deniseburn, identified as the Rowley Burn, seven miles south of the battlefield, that Cadwallon was killed.

The battle became known as Heavenfield and on the site a memorial church was built. The Chapel of St. Oswald, rebuilt in 1737, is thought to be in the same place and nearby were the fields in which the battle was fought. Opposite the Chapel, on the south side of the road, is a field called Mould's Close where the greatest slaughter took place and here many skulls and sword fragments have been dug up. According to Camden, when the Chapel of St. Oswald was being repaired in the time of Elizabeth, a silver coin of Oswald was found with his head on one side and a cross on the reverse.

The battle of Heavenfield was one of the decisive battles of English history. It finally decided the struggle between the Celts and the Anglo-Saxons and led to the complete conversion of Northumbria to Christianity, but to the Celtic not Roman version.

After a brief but brilliant reign Oswald was slain at the battle of Maserfield (said to be at Oswestry – Oswald's tree – Shropshire) in 642, his victor being the pagan king of the Mercians, Penda.

BATTLE OF CARHAM (833 A.D.)

The village of Carham lies on the very edge of Northumberland, almost on the banks of the Tweed. "In the 33rd yere of Ecbright", says Leland, "the Danes arrived at Lindisfarne, and fought with the English at Carham, when eleven Bishops and two English Countes were slayne, and a great numbre of people". A field to the south of the village is supposed to mark the site. This was one of the numerous battles which occurred during the period of the Danish invasions. It is only fair to mention that some historians place it not at Carham but in one of the southern counties.

BATTLE BRIDGE (875 A.D.)

There is a tradition that about the year 875 the Danes who had landed on the Northumbrian coast advanced up the Aln, plundering as they went. Four miles east of Whittingham they were met by the Saxons who lived in the valley. A bloody battle ensued in which the Saxons were defeated and the Edlingham burn is said to have run red with blood for three days and three nights. A hamlet near the spot is still called Battlebridge.

BATTLE OF BRUNNABURG (935 A.D.)

This battle between Athelstan and the Danish Chief, Anlaf, is often said to have been fought near Brinkburn. However, there is not the slightest evidence to prove the battle was fought anywhere in Northumbria.

BATTLE OF CARHAM (1018 A.D.)

A quarter of a mile to the north east of Wark is the site of an important battle which was fought in 1018 between Malcolm, king of Alban (Scotland), supported by Eugenius the Bold, king of the Strathclyde Brythons, and Uchtred, Earl of Northumberland. The English earl had called up the whole male population between the Tees and Tweed, including the old men who normally would not be called to service, but his army was almost totally destroyed. Bishop Aldhun is said to have died of grief at the deaths of so many of the children of St. Cuthbert. The battle was called after Carham, three miles away, because Wark was then an insignificant hamlet. The battle had one historic result – it seems to have established the Tweed as the boundary between the eastern marches of England and Scotland.

3

BATTLES OF DURHAM (1069 A.D.) and GATESHEAD (1081 A.D.)

After the defeat and death of Harold, at Hastings, William advanced north. The Saxon bishop of Durham, Egelwin, and the Earls Edwin and Morcar swore allegiance to him at York. But the northern provinces were still not completely under William's control and Robert Comyn, a Norman noble, was given the task of subjugating them. When he entered the bishopric he was warned by Egelwin that the people would not submit to acts of severity. The haughty Norman treated the warning with contempt and executed a few unarmed men as a warning. When he entered the city of Durham he was so confident of his strength that he scattered his soldiers among the inhabitants. Let A. Thierry (writing in 1825) continue the story:-

"Night came; and the men on the banks of the Tyne then lighted, on the heights, the fires which were to serve them as signals. They assembled in great numbers, and made all speed towards Durham. At daybreak they had arrived at the gates, which they broke; and the Normans were assailed on all sides in the streets, of the turnings of which they were ignorant. They attempted to rally at the episcopal house, where their count had taken up his quarters; they barricaded it, and defended it for some time, discharging their arrows upon the Saxons from above; but the latter terminated the conflict by setting fire to the house, which was entirely consumed, with those who had shut themselves up in it. Robert Comine was among the dead; he had brought with him twelve hundred horsemen in full armour, and it is not precisely known how many servants-at-arms and foot soldiers accompanied them. This terrible defeat made such an impression upon the Normans, that numerous forces sent to take vengeance for the massacre, having advanced as far as Elfertan, now Allerton, at an equal distance from York and Durham, being seized with panic, refused to proceed any further. It was rumoured that they had been struck with immobility by a supernatural force, through the power of a saint named Cuthbert, who was interred at Durham, and protected the place of his repose . . ."

"The defeat was not allowed to pass with impunity. William himself led the army of revenge. Everything in his path was destroyed, the crops burnt, the cattle butchered, the villages razed to the ground and the people slaughtered. The priests fled from Durham and took refuge on Lindisfarne. Resistance in the north was over, "the end of liberty according to the English, of rebellion according to the Normans. On both sides of the Humber, the cavalry of the foreign king, his counts, his bailiffs, and his couriers, thenceforward travelled unmolested on the roads and through the towns; famine, like a faithful companion of the conquest, followed their footsteps."

"Eventually the religious and military powers in the north were invested in one man, Walcher of Lorraine, who combined the powers of the Bishop of Durham and the Earl of Northumberland. He was the first of the Prince Bishops. The English inhabitants suffered grieviously at the hands of Walcher and his officers. With the murder of a Saxon noble called Liulf their patience came to an end. A general council or assembly was held at Gateshead. The Northumbrians attended in large numbers 'to address humble and peaceful petitions to their judge. They asked reparation for the various wrongs which had been done them. "I will answer none of your complaints", said the bishop, "unless you first count me down four hundred pounds of the best money". Then the Saxon who spoke in the name of all the rest, asked permission to deliberate with them. They all retired for a moment, as if to hold a consultation, but immediately the orator, who was the chief of the plot, cried out in the English tongue, "Short rede, good rede! slay ye the bishop!". At this signal they drew their weapons, fell upon the bishop, and slew him, together with a hundred men, French or Flemish. Two English serving-men were alone spared by the conspirators, who respected in them the blood of their own nation. This popular insurrection extended as far as Durham; the Norman fort there was attacked; but the garrison being numerous and well provided with arms, resisted the Northumbrians, who lost courage, and dispersed after a siege of four days.' (Thierry).

BATTLE AT ALNWICK (1093 A.D.)

In the winter of 1093 Malcolm III of Scotland crossed the English border and pillaged the northern parts of Northumberland as far as Alnwick. The raid was in revenge for the insolent treatment he had received at the court of William Rufus to which he had gone to do homage for the lands he held in England. On St. Brice's Day, the thirteenth of November, his army was encamped on the high ground one mile north of Alnwick Castle.

Robert de Mowbray, governor of Bamburgh Castle, was then earl of Northumberland and the defence of the county depended on him. He was ably assisted by his steward, Morel, who happened to be Malcolm's godfather.

They were unable to engage in open combat with the vastly superior Scottish army but managed to attack them by surprise and throw them into confusion. Malcolm was slain and Edward, his son, mortally wounded. The story of his death is described in a monkish legend written long afterwards. The Chronicle of Alnwick Abbey tells us:

"Malcolm was there mortally wounded near a certain spring, leaving his own name to that spring even for ever. Hence that spring is called in the native English tongue, Malcomswell. This King Malcolm was wounded by Hamund, then constable of the said Eustace de Vescy, with a certain lance, on the point of which he had placed the keep of the castle of Alnwick for a pledge, as if placing the castle with all its inhabitants in subjection to Malcolm, king of Scotland. This deed being done, Hamund returned with a quick step, sound, unhurt, and whole, passing over a ford of water immensely great, and then by the divine will overflowing above measure, and leaving his own name to this ford; whence the ford where he passed over is called, in the native English tongue, Hammund's Ford from that day and thenceforward.".

(Eustace de Vescy only came into possession of the barony of Alnwick ninety-two years after Malcolm's death).

From an early period a cross stood on the spot where tradition says Malcolm was slain. Half a mile north of Alnwick, on the left of the road, are the ruins of St. Leonard's Hospital, founded between 1193 and 1216 by Eustace de Vescy for the Soul of Malcolm, King of the Scots.

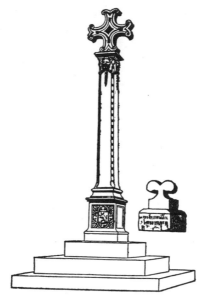

MALCOLM'S CROSS.
REMAINS OF THE OLD CROSS IN THE BACKGROUND.

Near the north side of the chapel is Malcolm's well where the monarch died. A quarter of a mile higher up the hill on the right hand side of the road is Malcolm's Cross, the traditional spot where he received his death wound. Part of the base and upper limit of the cross still survive in the plantation but a new one was erected in 1774 by Elizabeth, duchess of Northumberland, a descendant of Malcolm. It is ornamented "in the feeble style of the period" and inscribed on two sides with the following:-

MALCOLM III
KING OF SCOTLAND
BESIEGING
ALNWICK CASTLE
WAS HERE SLAIN
NOV. XIII, AN. MXCIII

K. MALCOLM'S CROSS
DECAYED BY TIME
WAS RESTORED BY
HIS DESCENDANT,
ELIZ: DUCHESS OF
NORTHUMBERLAND
MDCCLXXIV

On the other two sides are the lion of Scotland with Scottish thistles in the corner, and the Scottish thistle surmounted by a crown.

A SKIRMISH AT ALNWICK (1174 A.D.)

The skirmish at Alnwick in which William the Lion, King of Scotland, was taken prisoner, was militarily a minor affair but politically of great importance. Willam ascended the Scottish throne in 1165. Seven years later the eldest son of Henry II plotted with William to overthrow his own father, and in 1172 a Scottish army entered Northumberland for this purpose. But the incursion achieved little and a truce was arranged between the two monarchs. But two years later a new invasion was mounted by a large Scottish army, said to number 80,000, including many Flemish mercenaries. The chronicler tells us:

> *"The town of Belford was first attacked,*
> *Over all the country they scattered themselves;*
> *Some run to towns to commit their folly,*
> *Some go to take sheep in their folds,*
> *Some go to burn towns, I cannot tell you more;*
> *Never will such great destruction be heard spoken of.*
> *Then might you see peasants and Flemings who tie them,*
> *And lead them in their cords like heathen people.*
> *Women fly to the minster, each was ravished,*
> *Naked without clothes, she forgets there her property;*
> *Ah, God! why did William de Vesci not know it?*
> *The booty were rescued, nor would they have failed in it.*
> *They burnt the country; but God was a friend*
> *To those gentle peasants who were defenceless,*
> *For the Scots were not their mortal enemies;*
> *They would have beaten, slain, and ill-treated them all."*

Fantosme, 1167.

Although Northumberland was laid waste William achieved little. Failing to take Prudhoe Castle he moved north to besiege Alnwick. He had with him only 500 knights while the mass of his army pillaged the country around. They burnt the town of Warkworth and slew 300 men, women and children, who had taken refuge in the church of St. Lawrence.

Meanwhile, a small number of knights led by Odinel de Umfraville had advanced quickly from Newcastle to assist the defenders of Alnwick Castle. A spy they had sent in advance reported to them that William the Lion was encamped in a field a quarter of a mile west of the castle with only sixty knights. They were awaiting the arrival of their main forces and meantime had settled down to a meal. The English troops decided to attack:

7

"The king of Scotland was brave, wonderful, and old,
Before Alnwick he stood unarmed.
When these had once cried the war signal of Vesci,
And 'Glanville knights!' and 'Baliol!' likewise,
Odonel de Umfraville raised a cry of his own,
And this of Estuteville, a bold knight;
Then knew William that he was nearly betrayed,
Quickly he stirred himself, he was not disconcerted."

A brief struggle ensued and William and most of his attendants were taken prisoner.

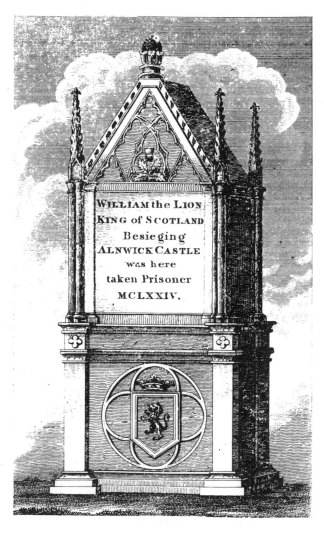

On the same day that William was captured Henry II was, as a penance, being flogged before the tomb of Thomas à Beckett in Canterbury Cathedral. A superstitious age immediately saw a connection between Henry's penance and one of the greatest events of his reign, the capture of Willaim the Lion, King of Scotland.

In the middle of the eighteenth century on the south side of Rotten Row a monument in the "pseudo-Gothic style" was erected to commemorate this event. Our engraving shows what it looked like. "Although not such as to gratify a refined taste, it was not without beauty, and was interesting as an illustration of the style of a period; and it is to be regretted that it has recently been taken down, and replaced by another erection entirely devoid of taste. This is a large square smoothed block of sandstone, nearly three feet in height, resting on two steps. A polished granite tablet is inserted into the face of the sandstone block; and on this is the inscription copied from the older monument.". G. Tate, 1866.

BATTLE OF HALIDON HILL (1333 A.D.)

In 1318 the Scots, under the leadership of Robert Bruce, gained possession of Berwick through the treachory, it is said, of one of the sentinels at the "Kow Gate", and for fifteen years it remained in their possession. In 1328 Edward III renounced all right to the dominion of Scotland in return for £20,000 to be paid by Scotland in compensation for damage done to England, and later in the same year his sister was married to David, son and heir of Robert Bruce. Great hopes were placed on this union and the princess received the appelation of *Make Peace*. But on the death of Robert Bruce Edward III decided to bring Scotland under his control. He began his campaign by laying siege to Berwick on the 12th of April, 1333. The Scots had prepared for this by provisioning the town and putting in a garrison of seasoned troops. Realizing the siege would take a long time Edward led the bulk of his army into Scotland, laying waste the country and capturing Edinburgh Castle. Returning to Berwick Edward established a complete blockade by sea and land, and the inhabitants suffered greatly.

In the meantime Lord Douglas raised a mighty army to relieve Berwick. In order to draw off Edward's army he marched south and invested Bamburgh Castle where the Queen was resident. But Edward did not raise the siege of Berwick since he knew Bamburgh was impregnable.

On 15th July the garrison at Berwick agreed to surrender in five days time and one of Seton's sons, he was deputy governor of the town, was handed over as a hostage to guarantee good faith. Edward already had taken prisoner his younger son. But Edward was afraid the town might be relieved before the surrender date of the 20th so he sent an ultimatum that the town must be surrendered immediately otherwise he would execute Seton's two sons in front of the rampart.

9

They biggit a gallows on hangie-dyke-neuk,
    And the hangman came there betyme;
The cock crow'd loudly o'er the muirs,
    'Seton's sonnes, 'tis matin pryme'.

The trumpets sounded out oure the Tweed,
    Wi' a blast o' deadly sound;
Auld Seton and wyfe goed up on the wa's,
    For theyre sonnes to death were bound.

They kennt the tread o' their gallant bairns,
    As they cam forth to die.
Richard, he mounted the ladder fyrst,
    And threw himself frae the tree.

William, he was his mither's pride,
    And he looked sae bauldly on;
Then kyst his brither's lyefless hands,
    When he fand the breath was gone.

He leaped from aff the bitter tree,
    And flouchtered in the wynd;
Twa bonnie flowers to wither thus,
    And a' for yae man's mind!

Oh! there was a shriek rose in the air,
    So wylde, so death-lyke gien;
A mother's wail for her gallant bairns,
    Sich sight was seldom seen.

It called the grey gull frae the sea,
    For he wist his mate had spake.
Never a mither in city walled,
    Wi' a heart that wadn't break.

Near the Royal Border Bridge is a small hill called *Hang-a-Dyke Neuk* where the execution is said to have taken place. "Moreover the remains of two human skulls are to be seen at this day in the poor-house of Tweedmouth, which the oldest and most respectable inhabitants of that village affirm to have been handed down from generation to generation as being the skulls of Sir Alexander Seton's two sons". (G. Fuller, 1799).

Lord Archibald Douglas now decided to engage in battle with Edward's forces. He marched across the Tweed and was confronted by the English army which occupied Halidon Hill, about two miles north west of Berwick. The armies were probably of equal numbers.

The battle started with a challenge to single combat by a Scots-man of gigantic stature called Turnbull who advanced accompanied by a great mastiff. The challenge was accepted by a Norfolk knight called Sir Robert Benhale. "The mastiff with the utmost ferocity darted forward, and the undaunted knight, receiving him with a skilful blow upon the loins with his sword, cut him in pieces. The Scotch hero advancing, Benhale with astonishing agility and adress, eluded the weighty blows aimed at him; and first cutting the left arm of his antagonist, then struck off his head."

The real battle now commenced. The Scotish army advanced boldly up the hill but once again the English archers proved decisive, the showers of arrows wreaking havoc among the close Scottish ranks. The English spearmen and men at arms followed up this advantage and the Scottish army fled in panic. The slaughter was dreadful and although the numbers are unreliable it is clear thousands of the Scots, including their commander, lay dead on the field of battle. The battle of Halidon Hill was long remembered as one of the greatest disasters in Scottish history. The immediate surrender of Berwick followed. Edward took hostages from the leading families but to be sure of the loyalty of the town encouraged many English merchants and tradesmen to settle there.

BATTLE OF NEVILLE'S CROSS (17th October, 1346)

Before dealing in detail with the battle of Neville's Cross we will briefly describe the Scottish army and soldiers and survey the main invasion routes into Durham. The Scots could advance into the Palatinate by the direct route through Northumberland, by-passing the static castles of Norham, Berwick, Alnwick and Bamburgh, but having to make the difficult crossing of the river Tyne or they could take the west route. Here they would march through Cumberland to Hexham and then had the choice of the valleys of the Browney or Wear for their further progress. The usual route was through Northumberland although in both the campaigns of 1327 and 1346 the Scots entered Durham from the West.

The Scottish army in the fourteenth century was not an effective fighting machine, consisting mainly of poorly armed feudal levies who found it difficult to capture large castles or fortified towns. It was, however, very mobile and although Durham and Newcastle were perfectly safe the rest of the counties could be laid waste. The best description of this army is given by Froissart in his description of the 1327 invasion:

The Scots are a bold hardy race and much inured to war. When they invaded England they were all usually on horseback except the camp followers; they brought no carriages neither did they encumber themselves with army provisions. Under the flap of his saddle each man had a broad plate of metal; and behind each saddle a little bag of

East side of
Nevill's +
a mile south of Durham City
26·10·97

oatmeal, so that when occasion needed cakes were made of oatmeal
and baked upon the plates; for the most part however they ate the
half soddened flesh of the cattle they captured and drank water.

In that campaign the Scots were able to lay waste the Palatinate
and then escape north, avoiding battle with the superior forces of
Edward III. The English king had to offer a substantial reward for
anyone who could even find the Scottish army.

In 1345 Thomas Hatfield became Bishop of Durham. The
following year King David of Scotland, who was in alliance with
the king of France, invaded England. Advancing through Cumberland his troops reached Hexham. They sacked the Priory but spared
the town, hoping to use it as a store-house for their plunder. After
crossing the rivers Tyne and Derwent David halted at Ebchester
and meeting no opposition advanced to Beau repaire (Bearpark),
three miles west of Durham. It was a manor of the Prior of Durham
set in a large walled park. Since David's visit it has been a ruin.

Meanwhile a large army was mustering under the command of
the northern nobility. They numbered near 16,000 men of whom
many were well armed and there were numerous trained archers.
On the 16th of October the English forces camped in Auckland
Park, and next day moved to Merrington from which place the
Scottish army was under observation in the hills west of Durham.
Moving slowly to "Fery on the Hill" the English surprised a large
foraging party under Sir William Douglas and pursued them as far as
Sunderland Bridge, the Scots losing 500 men. Reaching the safety of

12

Map of Durham by Thomas Jeffery, 1768

the Scottish army Douglas advised the king to avoid battle and retreat to the hills. From Sunderland Bridge the English army, in battle order, moved slowly to the moors near Neville's Cross. They had the rivers Dearness and Browney on their left flank and Durham and the River Wear on their right. The two armies joined battle on the Red Hills, a piece of broken ground on the banks of the Wear. The Scots were in three divisions, one under the king, one under the High Steward, the third under the Earl of Moray with Sir Willam Douglas. The English were also in three divisions, one under Lord Percy, the second under Lord Neville and the third commanded by Sir Thomas Rokeby. But the English also had in reserve, hidden in one of the hollows of the Red Hills, a strong body of cavalry under Edward Baliol. On a hill called the Maiden's Bower the Prior and many monks carried the holy cloth (the corporal or corporax which St. Cuthbert used to cover the chalice in the eucharistic service) on a spear. Other monks prayed from the tower of the Cathedral looking in the direction of the battle which was being fought.

The engagement started as usual with the English archers in front inflicting heavy casualties on the Scots. The High Steward's division then advanced, driving the archers through Percy's men whom they threw into confusion. But the advantage the Scots now had was lost when the reserve cavalry under Edward Baliol suddenly attacked and drove the High Steward's division off the field. Meanwhile the King had engaged Lord Neville but Lord Baliol, refraining from pursuing the High Steward's men attacked the royal division on the flank. The Scottish army was now in utter confusion. The king fled but was captured by John Copeland, a Northumbrian knight, while hiding beneath Aldin Grange bridge. This old stone bridge of one arch over the Browney, one mile from Neville's Cross, can still be seen. The third division was now attacked by the entire English army and, hampered by walls and ditches, was cut to pieces. The slaughter was dreadful and only remnants of the troops escaped.

The victory of Neville's Cross is said to have been commemorated by the erection of a cross whose mutilated remains are shown on the drawing made in 1885. We read:

On the west side of the city of Durham, where two roads pass each other, a most notable, famous, and goodly cross of stone work was erected to the honour of God, for the victory there obtained in the field of battle and known by the name of Nevil's Cross and built at the sole cost of the Lord Ralph Nevill, one of the most excellent and chief persons in the said battle. Also in token and remembrance of the battle of Durham, and to the perpetual memory and honour of the said Lord Nevill and his posterity for ever, it was termed by the title and name of Nevil's Cross, as above-said, and so did remain – till the year 1589, in the night-time the same was broken down and defaced by some lewd, contemptuous and wicked persons, thereto encouraged (as it seemed) by some who loved Christ the worse for the Crosse sake, as utterly and spightfully contemning all ancient ceremonies and monuments.

However there is much evidence to suggest a cross was there before the battle. On Thomas Jeffery's map of 1768 can be seen two other crosses in the vicinity, Phillip's Cross and Charly's Cross. The cross which Lord Neville is said to have set up was an elaborately carved structure. The pillar affixed to the octagonal base shown in our 1885 drawing is on part of the original cross, but appears to have been placed there early in the eighteenth century. Lord Neville, for his part in the battle, was allowed burial in Durham Cathedral, the first layman to be granted this honour. King David was released the next year on a ransom of 100,000 marks but the money was never paid.

NEVILLE'S CROSS, 1885.

The plague came to Scotland about this time and along with the battle of Neville's Cross brought peace to the Borders for many years.

BATTLE OF OTTERBURN (1388 A.D.)

The battle which has made Otterburn so famous was fought 19th August, 1388. The battle itself was of no importance, a useless carnage which had no military or political results. However the ballad singers have made the fight memorable with the romance they have created around it in their magnificent poetry.

15

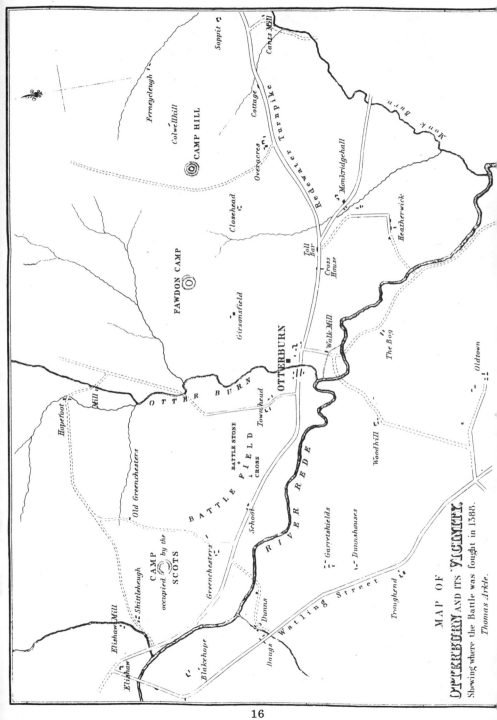

MAP OF
OTTERBURN AND ITS VICINITY.

Showing where the Battle was fought in 1388.

Thomas Arkle.

James, Earl of Douglas, had ravaged Northumberland and Durham with an army of 4,000 men. On his return he had challenged Sir Henry Percy (Hotspur) before the gates of Newcastle and then marched to Ponteland where he had burnt the castle. Proceeding north he reached Otterburn and bivouacked one and a half miles further up the valley in an old British camp. Meanwhile Sir Henry

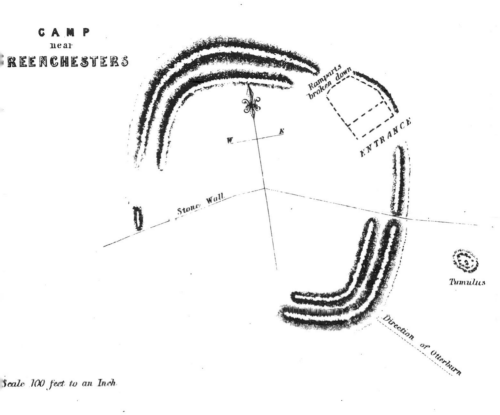

Percy had followed him from Newcastle with a superior force of 600 spearmen and 8,000 infantry. He reached Otterburn at night. Although his men were weary after their long march he decided to attack the Scots by moonlight. Mistake followed mistake. Instead of attacking the main Scottish troops the English, due to the darkness, made their main onslaught on the area occupied by the camp followers. A fierce battle developed as the Scots seized their chance and attacked the English flanks with their main forces. Douglas was killed, Percy was captured and the English forces routed. They lost almost 3,000 dead and 1,000 wounded, while the Scots had only 100 killed.

17

Meanwhile the Bishop of Durham with 7,000 men was advancing from Newcastle to assist Sir Henry Percy but meeting fugitives from the battle his army fled back to Newcastle panic stricken. Obtaining reinforcements he once again marched north with 10,000 men. The Scots were still encamped in the same place and as the English approached they blew on the horns which each man carried "that it seemed as if all the devils in Hell had come thither to join in the noise, so that those of the English who had never before heard such were very much frightened." The bishop observed the enemy were in a well chosen and fortified encampment and declined battle, returning to Newcastle. The Scots then crossed the border, taking with them their booty and prisoners.

It would be superfluous to write at length on the famous ballads which commemorate the battle of Otterburn, so much has already been written concerning the historical facts of the poems and their artistic merits. Ballad poetry is one of the glories of Northumberland. The earliest version called the *Hunting a' the Cheviat* is undoubtedly Scottish in origin and the best. It was of this ballad that Sir Philip Sidney wrote in his "Discourse of Poetry" in the following words:

"I never heard the old song of Piercy and Douglas, that I found not my heart more moved than with a trumpet; and yet it is sung by some blind crowder with no rougher voice than rude stile; which being so evil apparelled in the dust and cobweb of that uncivil age, what would it work trimmed in the gorgeous eloquence of Pindar."

The English ballad of *Chevy Chase* is a more polished version and is better known. Here are extracts from both versions:

It fell about the Lammas tide,
 When the mui-men win their hay,
The doughty Douglas bound him ride
 Into England to drive a prey.

He chose the Gordons and the Graemes,
 With them the Lindsays, light and gay;
But the Jardines waid not with them ride,
 And they rue it to this day.

And he has burned the dales of Tyne,
 And part of Bambroughshire,
And three good towers on Reidswire fells
 He left them all on fire.

And he marched up to Newcastle,
 And rode it round about;
"O wha's the lord of this castle?
 Or wha's the lady o't?"

18

A Douglas! A Douglas!

The Scottish Spearmen
closing in;
a Douglas!
a Douglas!

But up spake proud Lord Percy then,
  And O but spake hie!
"I am the lord of this castle,
  My wife's the lady gay."

"If thou art the lord of this castle,
  Sae weel it pleases me!
For ere I cross the Border fells
  The tane of us sall die."

He took a lang spear in his hand,
  Shod with the metal free,
And for to meet the Douglas there
  He rode right furiouslie.

But O how pale his lady looked,
  Frae off the castle wa',
When down before the Scottish spear
  She saw proud Percy fa'!

"Had we twa been upon the green,
  And never an eye to see,
I wad ha' had you, flesh and fell,
  But your sword shall gae wi' me.

"But gae ye up to Otterbourne
  And wait there dayis three;
And if I come not ere three dayis end,
  A fause knight ca' ye me."

"The Otterbourne's a bonnie burn,
  'Tis pleasant there to be;
But there is naught at Otterbourne
  To feed my men and me.

19

"The deer rins wild on hill and dale,
  The birds fly wild from tree to tree;
But there is neither bread nor kale
  To fend my men and me.

"Yet I will stay at Otterbourne,
  Where you shall welcome be;
And if ye come not at three dayis end,
  A fause lord I'll call thee."

"Thither will I come," proud Percy said,
  "By the might of Our Ladye!"
"There will I bide thee" said the Douglas,
  "My troth I plight to thee."   *Scottish Version*

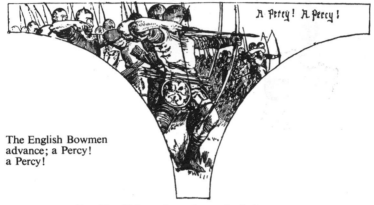

A Percy! A Percy!

The English Bowmen
advance; a Percy!
a Percy!

Our English archers bent their bowes,
  Their hearts were good and trew;
Att the first flight of arrowes sent,
  Full four-score Scots they slew.

Yet bides Erle Douglas on the bent,
  As Chieftain stout and good.
As valaint Captain, all unmov'd
  The shock he firmly stood.

His host he parted had in three,
  As Leader ware and try'd,
And soon his spearmen on their foes
  Bare down on every side.

Throughout the English archery
  They dealt full many a wound:
But still our valiant Englishmen
  All firmly kept their ground:

And throwing strait their bows away,
  They grasp'd their swords so bright:
And now sharp blows, a heavy shower,
  On shields and helmets light.   *English Version*

20

At Wallington Hall in Northumberland William Bell Scott painted a series of murals depicting the story of Chevy Chase. They are reproduced in full in the booklet "Scenes from Northumbrian History".

On the battlefield at Otterburn stands Percy's Cross, a pointed pillar about ten feet high which stands among a plantation of firs, north of the main road. The story of this cross is rather confused. About 150 yards east of the present cross once stood a monument called the *Battle Stone*. It is marked on Armstrong's map of 1769 and an engraving of it is here reproduced. It was only three feet in length resting in a socket. In 1777 the turnpike road from Otterburn to Redesdale was built and the Duke of Northumberland offered to build a memorial to the battle near the road. However Mr. Henry Ellison of Otterburn who owned the land thought the Duke might use this as an excuse to claim the ground and said he would build one himself. He chose a spot within view of the highway. A circular pedestal of rough masonry was built to the height of five feet in the centre of which the socket of the old Battle Stone was placed. Instead of a new shaft an old architrave from the kitchen fireplace at Otterburn Hall was used. Two bits of iron near the bottom of the shaft were probably used as hooks when it formed part of the fireplace. The erection was completed by placing on its top another stone tapering to a point. The old shaft from the old Battle Stone may be the stone in the porch of Otterburn Church.

Cross on the Battle Field near Otterburn.

BATTLE STONE REMOVED IN 1777.

21

BATTLE OF HOMILDON HILL (14th September 1402)

The battle of Homildon or Humbleton Hill was fought on 14th September, Holyrood Day, 1402. It was a border battle with important consequences. At the time there was a truce between England and Scotland but the Borderers paid little heed to it. George, Earl of March, had taken refuge with the Earl of Northumberland and assisted him in ravaging the lands of his arch enemies, the Douglases. A number of minor skirmishes took place in one of which, at Nesbit Moor, Sir Patrick Hepburn was slain, along with other Scottish knights.

To revenge his death the Earl of Douglas gathered a large army, said to be 10,000 strong, led by most of the Scottish nobility. They laid waste Northumberland as far as the gates of Newcastle and then set out on their return to Scotland with a vast quantity of booty. They encamped near Wooler but found their retreat cut off by the English forces under the Earl of Northumberland and his son Sir Henry Percy (Hotspur).

The Scots took up their position on the lower slopes of a hill to the west of Wooler called Humbleton. It was a fatal decision since they were exposed to the fire of the English archers, who occupied higher ground. Before they could engage in battle with the English men at arms the archers had inflicted grievous losses on them. The ballad singers tell us that Sir John Swinton – "a doughty knight as ever Scotland bred" – and Adam of Gordon, another Berwickshire baron, who had been mortal enemies up to now, became reconciled in this dire extremity and together led the Scottish nobility in a desperate effort to break through the English ranks.

> *Like two huge rocks on Braemar's brow,*
> *When loosen'd from their bed,*
> *That thunder down and overthrow*
> *The pines that crown the glade.*
>
> *Thus they, through ranks, the Earl of March,*
> *And the bold Percies sought,*
> *And blood and carnage mark'd their path,*
> *Where'er they stept and fought.*
>
> *At length they're wi' their gallant train,*
> *By numbers compass'd round,*
> *And fighting fall on heaps of slain,*
> *And stain with gore the ground.*
>
> *So did these valiant chieftains fall,*
> *Who lived in mortal strife;*
> *But lock'd in one another's arms,*
> *Dear friendship closed their life.*

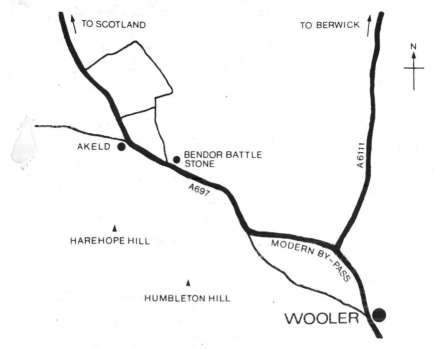

Site of Battle of Humbleton Hill 1402

The charge was a failure. Almost every man was slain or captured. The greatest slaughter took place on Red Riggs, the steep fields which lie to the west of the main road and since then many skulls and bones have been turned up by the plough. The remnants of the Scottish army were pursued to the Tweed where many hundreds were drowned. A stone, the Bendor Stone, in a field to the east of the road is said to commemorate the battle but it may be of an earlier date.

The prisoners taken were numerous and important, including the Earl of Douglas, who was severely wounded, and more than eighty knights and nobles. The Percys quarrelled with the king over the prisoners. Percy wanted to ransom them, as was customary, but the king wished to retain them in order to strengthen his hands in his negotiations with Scotland. The Earl of Northumberland and his sons then decided to move against King Henry. They made a secret agreement with the Scots and the Welsh to put Mortimer on the throne in place of Henry IV. Douglas and Percy were now united.

The Douglas and the Hotspur, both together, were confident against the world in arms.

The Scottish and Northumbrian armies marched towards Wales to join with the army of Glendower on the Welsh borders. But they were intercepted by the King at Shrewsbury where he inflicted a decisive defeat on them. Douglas fought like a demon. Shakespeare makes Hotspur say:

O, Douglas, hadst thou fought at Homildon thus,
I never had triumphed upon a Scot.

But soon Hotspur lay dead.

The noble Scot, Lord Douglas, when he saw
The fortune of the day quite turn'd from him,
The noble Percy slain, and all his men.
Upon the foot of fear, fled with the rest;
And, falling from a hill, he was so bruised,
That the pursuers took him.

Shakespeare's Henry IV Part 1 opens with the news of the battle of Homildon and this perhaps is why the conflict is still remembered today.

BATTLE OF HEDGLEY MOOR (1464)

In the year 1464, during the Wars of the Roses, James III of Scotland had sent ambassadors to negotiate with Edward IV at York. The Lancastrians had long relied on Scotland as a base and the success of these negotiations would have been serious for them. Lord Montague was sent north to escort the ambassadors through Northumberland. The Duke of Somerset tried to ambush him near Newcastle. Montague had only a small force, "four score spears and bows too," but he managed to evade the encounter. Before proceeding farther north Montague increased his forces and when his path was barred at Hedgley Moor he was sufficiently strong to destroy the Lancastrian troops and kill their leader, Sir Ralph Percy.

This meeting was upon St. Mark's day (April 25th) and that same day was Sir Ralph Percy slain. And when that he was dead, all the party was discomforted and put to rebuke. And every man avoided and took his way with full sorry hearts.

Sir Ralph was the second eldest of the nine sons of the Earl of Northumberland and an important supporter of the Lancastrian cause. Legends soon gathered around his death. Before the battle he was warned by a soothsayer of his imminent death which would be caused by the desertion of the Lords Hungerford and Ros. He ignored the warning and continued to trust his friends, who are said to have deserted him on the field of battle. According to tradition his dying words were "I have saved the bird in my bosom" which enigmatic sentence is supposed to mean he had kept his oath and promise to Henry VI. A strange claim from a man who had twice sworn allegiance to Edward IV.

24

Two ancient monoliths near the battlefield are called *Percy's Leap*. They are thirty feet apart and are supposed to mark the distance of his "leap" which he made when mortally wounded. These stones were probably erected hundreds of years before the Percy family came to England. Half a mile to the south is a stone called "Percy's Cross". It is a four sided pillar on a round pedestal bearing on its sides the arms of Percy and other heraldic insignia. It stands in a field east of the high road from Morpeth to Wooler, sixty yards off, and a little to the north of the twenty-first milestone.

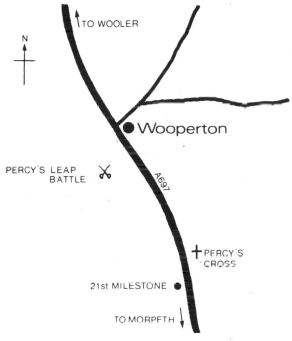

Battle of Hedgley Moor 1464

The stone was probably raised by Sir Ralph's nephew who, after a period of exile in Scotland, became the fourth Earl of Northumberland. Tradition says that annual games of football and cudgel playing were held here.

Nearby is a well which is sometimes called Percy's Well but its true name, as shown on an old estate map, is Sir James' Well.

Two ballads commemorate the battle – *The Battle of Hedgley Moor* by Frederick Sheldon, and *The Legend of Percy's Cross* by James Service.

Percy's Cross

BATTLE OF HEXHAM (15th May, 1464)

The battle of Hexham ended the four year war between Henry VI and Edward IV with the complete defeat of the Lancastrian forces. It was a battle of great importance.

After his defeat at the battle of Towton (1461) Henry VI and his wife, Margaret of Anjou, fled into Scotland. Here they were welcomed by the Scottish regency and the Queen-dowager, Mary of Gueldres. An army, mainly of Borderers, was raised to help them but since such troops only fought for plunder the Yorkists realised they could not be relied upon except for limited operations. Queen Margaret therefore crossed over to France in order to obtain French troops and money to assist the campaign.

Early in 1464 a truce was being negotiated between England and Scotland and the Lancastrians realised they would eventually lose Scottish support. In the north they only held castles in Northumberland. These included the coastal fortresses of Alnwick, Bamburgh, and Dunstanburgh and three castles in the Tyne valley, Bywell, Hexham and Langley.

On the 15th of April 1464 Lord Montague, one of the Yorkist commanders, met a detachment of the Lancastrians under the command of Sir Ralph Percy at Hedgley Moor, near Wooler, and routed them (see pages 25-27). The Lancastrian cause was now in complete decline. Most of Henry's supporters would only fight for personal gain and there was little money available. Although the northern counties, outside the towns, was mainly sympathetic to the Lancastrians the king had not the financial resources to raise large levies from among them.

After Hedgely Moor Henry VI seems to have moved to Tynedale. The story that the Yorkists found his helmet *cum corona et gladio*, when they captured Bywell, is probably true.

Lord Montague left Newcastle in early May and advanced up the Tyne towards Hexham. As soon as the king heard of his advance he fled westwards leaving his troops to fight alone. He was later captured (in July) near Clitheroe in Lancashire. Montague's advance was unopposed. He seems to have marched along the north bank and crossed the Tyne either at Bywell or Corbridge. The Lancastrians barred his way to Hexham at the passage of the Devil's Water above Dilston. They were outnumbered and fled after a very brief encounter. The battle, although of great importance, was a mere skirmish. Their leader, Somerset, was captured and executed in Hexham the same day. Lord Tailbois was captured while hiding in a pit near Newcastle. We are told that *he hadde moche mony with hym, bothe golde and sylvyr, that shulde hav gone unto King Harry: and yf it had come to Harry, lat kynge of Ingelonde, hyt wolde have causyd moche sore sorowe, for he had ordynyd harneys and ordenance i-nowe, but the men wolde not go one fote with hym tylle they had mony.* Ros, Molins, Hungerford, Findern and two others whose names are unknown were beheaded on the Sandhill in Newcastle.

The battle, in most of our local histories, is associated with the romantic story of Queen Margaret's escape. The story itself may be true but took place much earlier, probably at Norham. Margaret was abroad when the battle took place, and her husband, Henry VI, had fled four days earlier.

However, the story is so well known that we give it here as recounted in the Monthly Chronicle of 1888. 'The queen and the young prince took refuge in the adjoining forest. Hume, copying Monstrelet, tells us she was "beset, during the darkness of the night, by robbers, who, either ignorant or regardless of her quality, despoiled her of her rings, and jewels, and treated her with the utmost indignity." "The partition of this rich booty," the historian adds, "raised a quarrel among the robbers; and while their attention was thus engaged, she took the opportunity of making her escape with her son into the thickest of the forest, where she wandered for some time, overspent with hunger and fatigue, and sunk with terror and affliction. While in this wretched condition she saw a robber approach with his naked sword; and, finding that she had no means of escape, she suddenly embraced the resolution of trusting entirely for protection to his faith and generosity. She advanced towards him, and, presenting to him the young prince, called out to him, "Here, my friend, I commit to your care the safety of your king's son." The man, whose humanity and generous spirit had been obscured, not entirely lost, by his vicious course of life, was struck with the singularity of the event, was charmed with the confidence reposed in him, and vowed not only to abstain from all injury against the princess, but to devote himself entirely to her service." By this man's means, Margaret dwelt for some time hid in a wretched cave, which lies in an extremely secluded situation, beneath the southern bank of the little river that runs past Dilston Castle, exactly opposite to the Black Hill farmhouse. She was at last conducted to the sea coast, whence she made her escape to Sluys, in Flanders. From the Low Countries she passed to the court of her aged father at Aix, in Provence, where she lived several years in privacy and retirement, before returning to England to create new troubles.

The Northumbrian cave in which she lay concealed still retains the name of the Queen's Cave. The roof is supported by a pillar of rude masonry. According to tradition, the pillar forms part of a wall which divided the cave into apartments, for the accommodation of the devoted lady and her luckless son, the titular Prince of Wales, who was so cruelly murdered by King Edward and his myrmidons after the battle of Tewkesbury in 1471. According to a survey made in 1822, the cave does not exceed thirty-one feet in its greatest length and fourteen feet in breadth, while the height will scarcely allow of a person standing upright. In connection with Margaret, besides the cave, there is a small runner between Hexham and the Devil's Water, where it is said her horse fell, and which is still called "the Queen's Letch". '

The exact site of the battle is much disputed. The Ordnance Survey places it half a mile south of Linnel's Bridge, but Dorothy Charlesworth (Archaeologia Aeliana, 1952) suggests a more likely spot as half a mile north west of the bridge on Swallowship Hill.

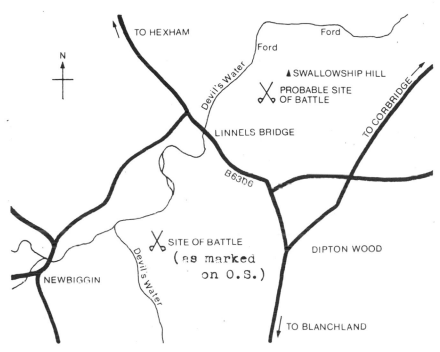

Battle of Hexham 1464

BATTLE OF FLODDEN (1513 A.D.)

The battle of Flodden was fought on the 9th of September, 1513 between James' IV of Scotland and Thomas Howard, Earl of Surrey. This was the last great conflict, apart from minor border raids between England and Scotland. On the 22nd of August, James IV crossed the Tweed near Coldstream with an army of 100,000 men. The object he had in view was to assist the French, whose lands were then being invaded by Henry VIII. James IV had finally decided on attacking England when he had received a ring from the Queen of France, together with 14,000 French crowns, to enable him to raise "an army and come three foot of ground, on English ground, for her sake". The public reason he gave was to avenge the death of Sir Robert Kerr, Warden of the East Marches, who was murdered at a border meeting in 1508 by the bastard Heron and two other Englishmen.

29

FOORD CASTLE
South Aspect

The castles of Norham, Ford, Etal and Chillingham were quickly taken. Having established a camp on the heights of Flodden, James made Ford Castle his headquarters for a week. The reason for his inactivity was undoubtedly the danger of advancing too far into Northumberland. "There is little or no reason to give credence to the old-wives tale that this inertion on the part of James was due to the fatal charms of dame Elizabeth Heron, the chatelaine of Ford".

In the meantime the Earl of Surrey, who was entrusted with the defence of England during Henry's absence in France, advanced northward calling upon the men of Northumberland and Durham to meet him at Newcastle. With an army of 30,000 to 40,000 men he advanced to Alnwick, Bolton and then to Wooler haugh. From here the English challenged the Scottish army to come down into the plain of Millfield to do battle. Finding the Scots were unwilling to give up their strong position Surrey marched to Barmoor Wood, four miles from Flodden.

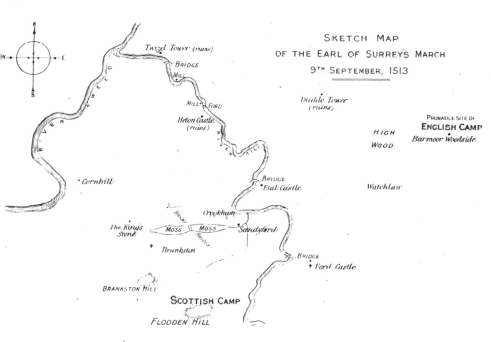

SKETCH MAP
OF THE EARL OF SURREY'S MARCH
9TH SEPTEMBER, 1513

Meanwhile many of the Scottish contingent had decided to return home so when the battle took place the armies were almost equal in numbers. However, the English army was in poor condition. During their march north the weather had been very wet. Worse still "there was little or no wine, ale, nor beer for the people to be refreshed with but all the army for the most part were enforced and constrained of necessity to drink water". The Scottish army, on the contrary, was well provisioned and had been resting for several days.

31

Early in the morning of the 9th Surrey left his camp and with his vanguard crossed the bridge at Twizel while the rearguard crossed at the ford near Heton Castle. The scene is thus described by Sir Walter Scott.

> "From Flodden ridge
> The Scots beheld the English host
> Leave Barmoor Wood, their evening post
> And heedful watched them as they crossed
>   The Till by Twizel Bridge.
> High sight it is, and haughty, while
> They dive into the deep defile;
> Beneath the caverned cliff they fall,
> Beneath the castle's airy wall.
>   By rock, by oak, by hawthorn tree,
> Troop after troop are disappearing;
> Troop after troop their banners rearing,
>   Upon the eastern bank you see.
> Still pouring down the rocky glen,
>   Where flows the sullen Till,
> And rising from the dim-wood glen,
> Standards on standards, men on men,
>   In slow procession still,
> And sweeping o'er the Gothic arch,
> And pressing on in ceaseless march,
>   To gain the opposing hill."

James has often been accused of military incapacity because he failed to attack the English as they were crossing the Till. But there were strong reasons why he should maintain his strong position at Flodden. To the north of Branxton was a large swamp which the Scots thought would be a serious obstacle for the English army. However part of the English forces skirted the moss and the remainder crossed by "Branx Bridge" a crossing unknown to the Scots. Realising that the enemy were making for Branxton Hill, which was as strong a position as Flodden and would cut off his escape into Scotland, James ordered the camp refuse to be set on fire and taking advantage of the dense smoke which a south-easterly breeze blew over the whole ridge, he transferred his forces to Branxton ridge. The plan of the battle shows the disposition of the forces.

The battle started with an artillery duel. As soon as the Scottish guns opened fire the men of Tynemouth and Bamburghshire, who were in Dacre's rearguard, fled, followed by Edmund Cheshire's followers who resented not being led by a Stanley. The English artillery was, however, superior and used more effectively.

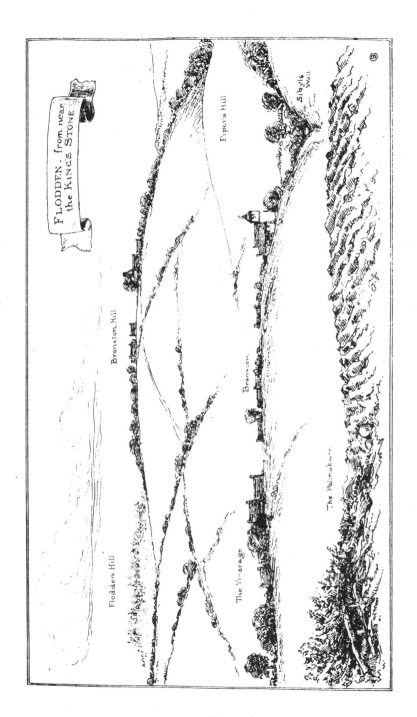

FLODDEN, from near the KINGS STONE

Branxton Hill

Piper's Hill

Sibyl's Well

Flodden Hill

Branxton

The Vicarage

The Palmekirk

The struggle was soon conducted at close quarters. The left wing of the Scots under the Earl of Huntley and Lord Home, "with long spears like Moorish pikes" put the English right wing, under Sir Edmund Howard, to flight. But the Scottish advance was halted by a band of north-countrymen led by John Heron, the bastard. The Scots under Crawford and Errol then engaged the Lord-Admiral and the English were soon in a serious position. The Scottish centre, led by James himself, and Surrey were then locked in combat and for a while the Scots were in the ascendant.

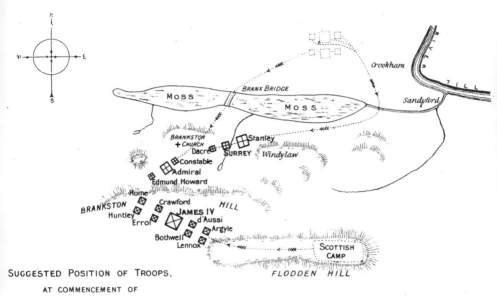

SUGGESTED POSITION OF TROOPS,

AT COMMENCEMENT OF

BATTLE OF FLODDEN.

The battle was, however, decided on the English left wing which was attacked by half naked highlanders under Lennox and Argyle. The English archers here wreaked havoc upon the clansmen and then advanced with the pikemen to the top of the ridge. Attacking the Scottish centre in the rear, a dreadful slaughter took place. The king and thirty of his noblemen were slain. The scene is described by Sir Walter Scott:

> "The English shafts in volleys hail'd:
> In headlong charge their horse assailed;
> Front, flank, and rear, their squadrons sweep
> To break the Scottish circle deep,
> That fought around their king.
> But yet, though thick the shafts as snow,
> Though charging knights like whirlwinds go,
> Though bill-men ply the ghastly blow,
>   Unbroken was the ring;

34

The stubborn spearmen still make good
Their dark impenetrable wood,
Each stepping where his comrade stood,
     The instant that he fell.
No thought was there of dastard flight;
Link'd in the serried phalanx tight,
Groom fought like noble, squire like knight,
     As fearlessly and well.
Till utter darkness closed her wing
O'er their thin host and wounded king.

At the crisis of the battle Lord Home refused to come to the king's assistance saying, "He does well that does for himself. We have foughten our vanguards, and have won the same, therefore let the lame do their part as well as we." Then joined by the moss-troopers of Tynedale and Teviotdale his men stripped the slain and plundered the baggage of *both* armies.

Fighting on a small scale continued next day until the rest of the Scottish army learnt of the death of their king. Among the booty captured by the English were seven beautiful cannon from Edinburgh Castle, called "The Seven Sisters".

RAID OF THE REIDSWIRE (1575)

At Carter Bar, 1,370 feet above sea level, is the boundary between England and Scotland.

The word Bar comes from the tollhouse which once stood on this spot when the turnpike was built in the eighteenth century. The word Carter comes from the Celtic "cart" meaning a hill. Carter Bar is a *swire*, or neck of land, connecting Catcleugh Shin and Arks Edge and was anciently called Reidswire. The land up here is bleak indeed. Tomlinson relates how an old carrier who was asked what he thought of the weather up there replied "Hoot, man, hoot; the very de'il himsel' wadna bide there half an hour unless he was tethered!"

In 1575 the last battle between England and Scotland took place here, a fight commemorated in the famous ballad 'The Raid of the Reidswire'.

It was the custom in the Middle Ages for the Wardens of the Marches on both sides of the Border to meet periodically to settle disputes and punish those who had commited crimes on both sides. In 1575 such a meeting took place between Sir John Forster, the English Warden, and Sir J. Carmichael, the Keeper of Liddesdale. For a while the business of the day was conducted peaceably. Then a dispute arose over the famous English freebooter named Farnstein. High words passed until the Tynedale men started the battle with a flight of arrows. The ballad tells the story:

35

Yett was our meeting meek eneugh
    Begun wi' merriment and mowes,
And at the brae aboon the heugh
    The clark sat down to call the rowes,*
    And some for kyne and some for ewes
Call'd in of Dandrie, Hob and Jock —
    We saw come marching ower the knowes
Five hundred Fenwicks in a flock.

With jack and speir and bows all bent,
    And warlike weapons at their will;
Although we were na well content,
    Yet, by my troth, we fear'd no ill.
    Some gaed to drink, and some stude still,
And some to cards and dice them sped;
    Till on ane Farnstein they fyled a bill,
And he was fugitive and fled.

Carmichael bade them speak out plainlie
    And cloke no cause for ill or good;
The other answering him as vainlie
    Began to reckon kin and blood
    He raise and raxed† him where he stood
And bade him match him with his marrows;
    Then Tindaill heard them reasun rude,
And they loot off a flight of arrows.

      * *Rolls*   † *Stretched*

In the ensuing babble the Scots were victorious, the English retreated for three miles leaving many dead and prisoners. However, a few weeks later the prisoners were released by the Scots to prevent a war developing between the two kingdoms.

This battle is still commemorated today. On the anniversary of the battle horsemen from Scotland and England meet here as a sign of the friendship that has existed between the two countries since the engagement. A special meeting was held in 1975 on the occasion of the 300th anniversary.

THE BATTLE OF NEWBURN (28th August, 1640 A.D.)

In 1640 the struggle between Charles I and the Scottish Covenanters laid the foundation for the English Civil War and the eventual over-throw of Charles. In August the supporters of the Solemn League and Covenant crossed the border under the command of General Leslie. Their numbers were estimated at 20,000 foot and 2,500 horse. The Scottish army passed through Wooler, Eglingham and Nether-witton, bearing flags with the words *For Christ's Crown and Covenant.*

As they marched they had "daily sermons from their ministers, prayers morning and evening under the canopy of heaven, to which they were called by beat of drum; besides reading of the Scriptures, praying, and psalm-singing, in every tent."

They reached Newburn on the north side of the Tyne. Here the river was fordable at two places, the nearest points to Newcastle. The Scots encamped on Heddon-law above Newburn whence there was a continuous descent to the Tyne. Coal could be found in abundance so great fires were built all about the camp. The English army, made up of 3,000 foot and 1,500 horse were drawn up on Stella Haugh, a meadow nearly one mile in length on the south of the river. At the two fords breastworks were built (traces of which were still visible less than 100 years ago).

The Scots, having the advantage of the higher ground above Newburn, could overlook all the English troops. On the 28th August the Scots placed their cannon in Newburn village, even using the church steeple, with their foot hidden among the houses, lanes and hedges. The battle started with an English musketeer hitting a Scottish trooper who was watering his horse in the Tyne. Leslie's troops replied with a heavy cannonade on the English redoubts. They were superior in numbers and discipline and by the time the tide had fallen, making the river fordable, the English had abandoned their major redoubt. A few hundred cavalry and musketeers crossed the river and before long the king's troops were in flight. The fight at Newburn hardly merits the title "battle". Clarendon, the historian of the royalist side, described it as "that infamous, irreparable rout". The disaster at Newburn was, however, a major defeat for Charles.

The Scots treated their prisoners with honour and soon released them. Meanwhile the English troops had retreated to Newcastle and Durham. At a meeting in Newcastle at midnight the same day Lord Strafford decided the city was indefensible and immediately marched south, leaving all the stores and munitions to the enemy. The Covenanters entered the city next day. Their victory at Newburn had given them control of Northumberland and Durham. Rushworth graphically describes the collapse of all resistance "at this time Newcastle and the coalmines, that had wont to employ 10,000 people all the year long, some working underground, some above, and others upon the water in keels and lighters, now not a man to be seen, not a coal wrought, all absconding, being possessed with a fear that the Scots would give no quarter; 400 ships using to be there often at a time in the river, not a ship durst come in; an hundred and odd coming to the mouth of the haven the day after the fight, and hearing the Scots had possessed Newcastle, returned all empty, and tradesmen in the town for some days kept their shops shut, many families gone, leaving their goods to the mercy of the Scots, who possessed themselves of such corn, cheese, beer, etc., as they found giving the owners thereof, or some in their stead, some money in hand, and security in writing for the rest, to be paid at four or six months' end, in money or corn; and if they refuse, said the Scots, such is the necessity of their army, that they must take it without security rather than starve. As for the City of Durham, it became a most depopulated place; not one for four days after the fight open; not one house in ten that had either man, woman, or child, in it; not one bit of bread to be got for money, for the king's army had eat and drank all in their march into Yorkshire; for the people durst not come to market, which made that city in a sad condition for want of food. At this time a letter came from the Lord Lieutenant-General, to bury or break every upper millstone, and drive and carry away all cattle and goods to a great distance, insomuch that most drove their cattle and sheep into Yorkshire, and removed most of their families thither also."

The Bishop of Durham, Morton, fled to his castle at Stockton and thence into Yorkshire and the See of Durham could now be considered temporarily ended. "The Dean of Durham fled in great haste, because he understood the Scots gave out that they would seize upon him as an incendiary for writing the king's large declaration against the Scots. All the rest of the clergy of Durham fled away also; and the Scots shortly after employed men to receive their rents and the rents of Popists, for the use of the Scottish army."

. . . such were the results of the skirmish at Newburn.

THE SIEGE AND STORMING OF NEWCASTLE (1644)

By 1643 the Civil War between Parliament and King Charles had reached a stalemate. This was ended by the alliance which Parliament made at the end of the year with Scotland whereby the Scottish army was thrown in on their side.

In January 1644, in a heavy snowstorm, the Scots army crossed the Tweed and entered Northumberland, thereby threatening to overrun those areas which so far had been under the undisputed control of the Royalist forces, for at this time in all the northern counties only Hull was still held for Parliament. Under the leadership of the Earl of Leven, a soldier of great experience and ability, the Scottish army of 20,000 men was a formidable force and the King's troops quickly retired as the Scots advanced, till they reached the gates of Newcastle.

Although four years previously Newcastle had surrendered to the Scots without a blow being struck, on this occasion Leven was surprised to find her in a posture of defence with the walls well repaired and manned and everything ready to withstand a siege if necessary.

After a small brush with the town's defenders Leven continued his march south, leaving a small force behind to cover the town. For a week or two he skirmished against the Royalist forces in Durham without any decisive engagement taking place. But Parliamentary successes in Yorkshire compelled the Marquis of Newcastle, who commanded the forces opposing Leven, to withdraw even south of Durham into Yorkshire, where he was still followed by Leven and the Scottish army.

Then on the 2nd of July the decisive battle of Marston Moor, which among other things sealed the fate of the city of Newcastle, was fought, and by the genius of Cromwell was made into an overwhelming victory for Parliament. To north country people the battle is well known because of the part played in it by the Whitecoats. While the Royalist cavalry fled at the charge of Cromwell's Ironsides the men of Northumberland stood firm and died where they stood. As one writer described the scene: "Once again Cavalier and Ironside fiercely charged, and once again victory remained with the Ironsides. The Cavaliers fled the field, while Newcastle's regiment of Whitecoats, a thousand brave Northumbrians raised out of his own tenantry, scorning to receive quarter or to fly, were all, save some thirty, cut down to a man."

Immediately following Marston Moor Leven returned north to continue the siege of Newcastle where beyond the inhabitants there were none left now to oppose him. Meanwhile a new Scottish army under the Earl of Callender had reinforced the troops left at Newcastle by Leven and was vigorously prosecuting the attack. To resist them was but a small force consisting of 1,700 men, made up of 800 of the train-band and some 900 besides, of "Voluntiers, prest-men, Coliers, Keill-men, and poore trades-men".

Callender after a short campaign in Durham took possession of Gateshead, from the banks of which he kept Newcastle under a steady bombardment which was replied to by guns mounted on the Half Moon Battery, and as soon as Leven arrived a bridge of boats was thrown across the river and the town was thus completely encircled, save for a gap where a fort at Shieldfield outside the walls still resisted. A vivid description of the action as it developed and the conditions of the opposing forces is given by a Scottish soldier who participated in the siege and published an account of it the following year. Here is an extract from William Lithgow's story:

"Now as for the manner of the common souldiers, lying here in their severall leagures, and in all parts about the towne, their mansions or domiciles, I meane their houts are composed, of turff, clay, straw, and watles. Where their halls, chambers, kitchines and cellars are all one; and yet the better sort (I mean their officers) are overshadowed with circulating pavillions, more ready to receive the blustring winde than the sinking rain. Then at last, all things being orderly done, and their batteries at sundrie advantages erected; then (I say) begun they to play with cannon and musket at other faces, and often also tempering their naked swords in other bloudy bodies: where courage cassiering despair, and valour desirous of honour, they exposed themselves unto all hazards and dangerous attempts: neither did they feare death (I meane our owne) more than an

auspicious fortune, for being clad with consorts, each provoked
another to the uttermost of extremities; and some of them esteeming
of the good cause, more than of their owne lives, reserved the one,
and lost the other. So also the inveterate enemie, making now and
then diverse sallies from towne (issuing at posterne gates) upon our
flanking trenches, engadged themselves into great jeopardies, and our
souldiers to as desperat a defence. Where indeed they both often
tasted of mutuall fatalitie; till in the end, the Lord Sinclairs Regiment,
desygned these debording hyrelings a narrower precinct; which was,
to keepe their falling bodies more safely within their sheltring walls,
which indeed they constrainedly observed. For the enemy within,
were more affrayed of the Lord Sinclairs souldiers without, then any
one regiment of the army lying about, and they had just reason,
recogitating seriously their sanguine blowes and fatall rancounters,
which they disdainfully felt."

Lithgow had a wholesome respect for the defences of Newcastle
which he describes as stronger than those of York, the walls being
"not unlyke to the walles of Avineon, but especially of Ierusalem.
Being all three decored about the battlements, with like quadrangled
turrets; the advantage resting onely upon Newcastle, in regard of
seventeen dungeon towers, fixt about the walles (and they also
wonderfull strong) which the other two have not". But of the inhabitants of the town he had a very poor opinion, lower indeed than
that of any other writer. Here is his extremely partisan description:
"As for the inhabitants resyding within, the richest or better sort of
them as seven or eight common knights, aldermen, coale merchants,
pudlers, and the like creatures are altogether malignants, most of
them being papists, and the greater part of all I say, irreligious
atheists. The vulgar condition being a mass of silly ignorants, live
rather like to the Berdoans in Lybia (wanting knowledge, conscience,
and honesty) than like to wel disposed Christians, plyable to religion,
civill order, or church discipline, and why? because their brutish
desires being onely for libertinous ends; avarice, and voluptuous-
nesse; they have a greater sensualitye, in a pretended formalitye,
than the savage Sabanucks with whom I leave them her engrossed."

Meanwhile the siege continued and the town being cut off from
supplies, hunger soon reared its head, and divisions began to develop
among the townsmen; while outside the Scots, assisted by colliers
from Benwell and Elswick, began to mine the town walls, while
batteries of guns bombarded the town preparatory to a final assault.

In London the battle at Newcastle was followed with intense
interest. Coal had there risen to famine prices and on the early
conclusion of the siege depended whether there would be any coal at
all that winter. That the town would be taken was a foregone conclusion; the question was how soon.

The Scottish commanders although pushing ahead their plans
for a grand attack entered into repeated negotiations with the Town
Council for an honourable surrender. On their terms being refused

Newcastle Town Walls under attack

they began to drop propaganda leaflets over the walls, having heard, perhaps with a certain amount of truth, that the poorer citizens wanted to give up the unequal struggle and were only kept going by the influence and pressure of Sir John Marley, the strongly Royalist Mayor. One of these propaganda leaflets – signed by a well-wisher of Newcastle – has come down to us. "I have been silent," the leaflet read, "waiting when you should have taken some course for your own happiness; but now seeing your distraction ever rife, if not timeously prevented, I could not but give you fair warning, and desire you both citizens and soldiers, for the preservation of your town, the safety of your persons, estates, and families, to think upon some way of speedy accommodation, and no question you shall meet with a very favourable hearing. It is no more wisdom nor honour, but extreme madness, any longer to hold out when the danger is present and certain, and when all your hopes of relief have now failed you."

Propaganda failing, the Earl of Leven sent his famous threat to destroy the spire of St. Nichol a sunless an immediate surrender was made. To this Sir John Marley, after placing his Scottish prisoners in the lantern of the tower, replied: "that they would upon no terms deliver up the town, but would to the last moment defend it. That the steeple of St. Nicholas' was indeed a beautiful and magnificent piece of architecture, and one of the greatest ornaments of their town, but yet should it be blown into atoms before ransomed at such a rate. That, however, if it was to fall it should not fall alone; that the same moment he destroyed the beautiful structure, he should bathe his hands in the blood of his countrymen, who were placed there on purpose either to preserve it from ruin, or to die along with it."

Further negotiations followed but it was clear that Sir John Marley was only playing for time and on the 19th October the last reply was sent to the Scots from Newcastle. It was in the form of an arrogant and sarcastic letter from the Mayor. It read as follows:-

"My Lord – I have received diverse letters and warrants subscribed by the name of Leven, but of late can hear of none that have seen such a man; therefore, to remove all scruples, I desire our drummer may deliver one letter to himself. Thus, wishing you could think of some other course to compose the differences of these sad distracted kingdoms than by battering Newcastle, and annoying us who never wronged any of you, for if you seriously consider, you will find that these courses will aggravate, and not moderate, distempers. But I will refer all to your own consciences, and rest, your friend,
John Marley"

Next morning under the cover of a heavy bombardment, a general attack started on the town, the mines were sprung and several breaches made. For two hours scenes of desperate fighting were witnessed but eventually the defenders were overpowered. A laconic report sent to the Lord High Chancellor of Scotland sums up the fighting. It tells how "my Lord Chancellor's regiment entered at a breach at Closegate, others entered by two mines at White Tower and Westgate, while two other mines were sprung and two more breaches made. Some houses were burned. They within the town made all the opposition they could on the walls and in the streets."

The whole town was now in the hands of the Scots save the castle to which Sir John Marley and other officers had fled. To most of the inhabitants the end of the siege and the slaughter must have been welcome since "there was such scarcity of victuals and ammunition, that it was considered that unless one-half of the people devoured the other, they could not have held out ten days longer."

For the next twenty-four hours the town, as was the custom in those days, was given over to plunder, "the whole army, commanded and uncommanded, observing King David's ancient rule, that they who stayed with the baggage and they that fought in the field should share in the plunder alike. For twenty-four hours they plundered, but without any great result. For the common soldiers being only able to plunder the common people (although they might have stretched out their hands further) had for the greatest part of them but small benefit, excepting only household stuff, as bed-clothes, linings, tanned leather, calf skins, men and women's apparel, pans, pots, and plates, and such like common things."

. In the castle things became so hopeless that after four days Sir John Marley and his friends surrendered unconditionally. When they came out to surrender a mob of the townspeople almost tore them to bits, since they looked upon them as the cause of the suffering they had undergone. Marley was then placed in the castle dungeon and although it was expected, that the hangman "would salute his neck with a blow of Straffords courtesey" he nevertheless managed to escape, on being taken to London, and went into exile.

In spite of the plundering Leven treated the townspeople with remarkable clemency, and once the town was properly in his possession prevented further pillage and slaughter. In fact Lithgow with his customary exaggeration remarked that considering the malicious obstinacy of Newcastle he was "ravished with admiration to behold, how in the heat of blood, and goaring slaughter, they got so soon mercy and quarters; that me thinketh there was not the like mercy shown in such a case, since the deluge of the world."

The loss of Newcastle was a great blow to Royalist hopes and their misfortunes were finally crowned when King Charles himself was held there as a prisoner by the Scots before being handed over to Parliament. The Stuart cause was so closely linked with that of Newcastle that we can appreciate the reasons with which they eventually invested the town with its motto, taken from the great siege, FORTITER DEFENDIT TRIUMPHANS.

INDEX